Full Circle:
Poetic Reflections on Self, Relationships, and Faith

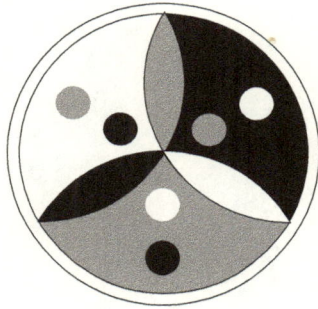

ISBN 9780615325613

CONTENTS

FAITH

SELF

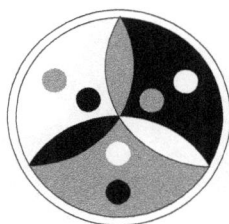

Where I'm From

I'm "comin' from where I'm from, I'm from".[1]
I'm from suburban parks and bike rides to friends' houses to play Nintendo.
I'm from city blocks that are becoming more urban.
I'm from neighborhood parks.
I'm from a dead end street that ends in opportunity.
I'm from where Black and White all have houses with nice yards, but are still
    divided by railroad tracks.
I'm from where an interracial couple is not odd.
I'm from one high school.
I'm from two middle schools.
I'm from where all schools hold students and teachers to the highest
    academic standards.
I'm from turnpike exits and Hebrew schools.
I'm from where having two cars and a three bedroom house still means
    hiding from the sheriff when the mortgage payment is late.
I'm from big business and trips to the big city.
I'm from the silhouette of the Empire State and the Statue of Liberty.
I'm from laundromats and main streets.
I'm from corner delis with 10 cent candies.
I'm from pizza for $1.25 a slice.
I'm from a bagel with a schmear.
I'm from come on mom, spaghetti again?!
I'm from Tahitian Treat and government cheese on toast bubblin'.
I'm from trips down south to grandma's house for fried chicken and
    collard greens.
I'm from sittin' on the front porch with country cousins playin',
    "I got that car".
I'm from summertime ending and heading back home.
I'm from two Black parents.
I'm from Fredrick Douglas and Sojourner Truth.
I'm from Booker T. Washington and Harriet Tubman.
I'm from playin' little league in 1985.
I'm from a basement full of mugs and coasters, holding Black faces, and titled
    "the Black Heroes of the Bicentennial", that dad couldn't sell in 1976.
I'm from hiding behind the couch when mom and dad argue.
I'm from weekend visits with dad and meeting his new girlfriend.

continued on next page

continued from preceding page

I'm from working summers with dad at his office.
I'm from moving around town, and out of town, and back to town.
I'm from the Ivy League.
I'm from a corner on the Southside of Chicago where a young brother asks
    me, "what you claiming?", because of how I where my hat.
I'm from education and introspection.
I'm from a birth in the garden.
I'm from a deceptive serpent.
I'm from generation after generation of prophet begging me to repent.
I'm from the great redeemer.
I'm from the crucifixion.
I'm from the resurrection.
I'm from faith, hope, and love.
I am from, the I Am, the Great I Am.
I am from realizing that I am from GOD.
And now you know that "I'm comin' from where I'm from, I'm from".[2]

---

[1] Hamilton, Anthony. (2003). From the song *Comin From Where I'm From*. On the album *Comin From Where I'm From*. So So Def Recorrdings.

[2] Ibid.

Who Am I?

I pray to love and be loved.

Everything is young, fresh, and new.
Every experience sends a rush of emotion.
Every touch is electric.
I do not think, I only feel.

I want candy.
I want to play.
I like video games.
Can I have some ice cream?

A mixture of daze and confusion.
A fleeting illusion, adrift in endless space.
I am a spec in the vastness of space and time.
One grain of sand on the beach of eternity.

I am an unstoppable giant.
Nothing can harm me.
No man can stop me.

About ten grey hairs in my beard now,
a few more on the crown of my head.
I wear them like a badge of honor.
Each one earned by progressing through the struggle.

I am battered.
I am weary.
The battle is nearing its end,
because I have God, I will be victorious.

I pray to love and be loved.

I Am Hip-Hop

I am hip-hop,
Biggie Smalls and Tupac,
Nas and Jay-Z,
Mos Def and Heavy D.

Old school and new,
LA to Brooklyn Zoo,
Heads start noddin',
when I roll through.

The snare,
the kick,
the boom and the bip,
the high hat,
I'm all that,
skills is mad phat.

As a kid studied peace,
growin' up in the east.
South Central as teen,
to serve them feens.
Got a little older,
skills got bolder,
hit the Chi-town,
now I'm a money folder,
The old school said *Chill*,
I'm still gettin' colder.

The beat, the lyrics,
the DJ and the mic.
All about love,
but I still feel spite.
Not spreadin hate,
but the guns do ignite;
when they hear my voice,
wildin' in the night.

continued on next page

30°

continued from preceding page

Where I'm headed next?
about to take over.
All around the globe,
like my name was Range Rover.
Spreadin' everywhere like a global pandemic,
you gave me the game now about to hem it.
Sew it,
keep it,
lock it all down.
Want to see me perform,
I'm comin' to your town.

You can feel the love,
witness the fight.
When's it all over?
No endin' in sight!

Real Talk

"Writin' in my book of rhymes all the words past the margin".[3]
Who startin'?
Who want beef?
I'ma keep it cookin',
and make sure that ish is sizzlin',
'til I'm makin' it cease.
All you brothers beefin' better be happy that I don't eat red meat,
or I would come out buckin',
but I'm a man of peace.
Shalom ya'll.
Still any MC steppin' is steppin' closer to downfall.
It's a slippery slope and my lyrics is dope.
Snorted, shot, or smoked they givin' all my people hope.
I'm like a Civil Rights leader workin' for the right to vote.
I feel hate,
but keep it movin' because I'm a man on a mission.
It ain't all about the money but I'm a be insistent,
that I get mine.
I will give it all away later,
but I gotta get it now to send a message to haters.

[3] Jones, Nasir. (1994). From the song *The World is Yours*. On the album *Illmatic*. Columbia Records.

Lunchtime Meeting

My neck tie tightens around my throat.
My watch binds my wrist.
My smartphone singes my hip.
My mind slips,
from the bureaucratic psycho-babble,
that spills from the mouth of my meeting facilitator.
Playa-hater.
Why can't you let a brother live,
like he is supposed to.
What makes you think I care.
I have a job to do,
and you ain't helpin'.
You got my attention,
teach me somethin'.
Broaden my horizons.
Blow my mind.
Don't waste my time.
What are "expections"?
Do you mean expectations?
Learn how to talk,
You just politicin',
lookin' forward to future elections.
Maybe it is my arrogance or my ego,
I don't know.
I do know,
I want you to speak with some common sense,
so we don't go in circles,
wasting time on trifles.
This earthly life is not eternal.
So I would rather use this finite time on something more educational or enjoyable.
The Lord knows I've tired,
but I can't take it no more,
so like the sun,
I RISE,
my butt out of this seat.
I'll check ya'll fools later,
I'm going to get something to eat.

Ph.D. Program

Another droning diatribe,
irrelevant to the survival of my tribe.
Trying to convince me and mine,
that she and hers are on my side.
A dull, faded glaze in her eyes.
She's hoping to get a piece of the pie,
some cash,
that's her big prize.
And doing it all the time,
in the name of helping,
the children.
Another expert.
Another Ph.D.
Another dead ear.
Another blind eye.
Another boring speaker,
who I ain't feelin'.
Who just ain't willin',
to spend the time.
To open her mind.
To spend even one little dime,
on anything that helps me and mine,
unless it is in pursuit of her prize.
I would call you Judas,
but you were never a disciple.
Just one of the masses.
Blind behind her glasses.
Given authority to teach classes.

continued on next page

continued from preceding page

While another child passes,
through the system of,
corruption,
dysfunction,
disillusion,
mass confusion,
pain,
suffering,
heartache,
poverty,
and neglect.
And you take "absolute zero" time to reflect,
on your part in it all.
Your trickle down makes us fall.
Down,
to the bottom of the barrel,
and we fight each other like crabs to get to the top.
Look!
Your 45 minutes are up!
Why don't you just stop!

Evening Meeting

Waiting, waiting, waiting.
Sedentary.
Ill-informed.
Dependent.
Passive.
Docile.
Weak.
Sleepy.
Dull.
No opportunities for production.
"Time keeps on slippin, slippin, slippin. Into the future".[4]
I hear and see,
but experience,
no activity.
Left to ponder.
When?
I can get in.
Get into the act.
All the world is a stage.
I wait in the wings.
I have no role.
No lines.
No possibilities.
Is this a life worth living?
What is my next task?
How do I get past the impasse, of inactivity?

[4] Miller, Steve. (1976). From the song *Fly Like an Eagle*. On the album *Fly Like an Eagle*. Capitol Records.

New Jersey Turnpike

Sirens sounded!
I was astounded!
And when I pulled over,
my car was surrounded!
What the heck are the police pulling me over for?
I was only driving 55.
I wasn't even close to havin' my foot on the floor,
but I guess I fit the description.
Now they're tellin' me to listen,
to their demands and orders.
I drop my head on the wheel and take two deep breaths,
in an attempt to prepare for this ordeal.
Hope these cops ain't thinking bout lynching me.
I know that is always a possibility.
Especially if you consider our history.

"HANDS OFF THE WHEEL AND IN THE AIR,"
with a tone of voice intended to scare,
or intimidate.
I know one thing about all of this,
I ain't gonna be no inmate.
I ain't goin' to jail.
I ain't payin' no bail.
I ain't commited no crimes,
so I ain't doin' no time.

"BOTH HANDS OUT THE WINDOW AND OPEN YOUR DOOR
    FROM THE OUTSIDE."
In the rearview I see guns drawn.
My heart skips a beat,
with the thought that they might try to use their heat.

continued on next page

continued from preceding page

"GET OUT OF THE CAR, PUT YOUR HANDS ON YOUR HEAD,
   AND WALK BACKWARDS TOWARD US."
What is this all about?
I was going to visit my man.
Good Lord please help me.
All I can do is put this in your hands.

"STOP!"

"LAY DOWN ON THE GROUND AND SPREAD OUT YOUR ARMS
   AND LEGS!"
This asphalt is freezing.
I think my knees are bleeding,
from trying to get down on the ground.
A knee in my back.
One on my neck.
My face scraped by the cold highway.
Barking sounds.
God, I beg of you please,
don't let them put that dog on me.
Can't they see that I didn't do anything?

The pain in my back interrupts my thoughts.
Hands grope my body in search of contraband.
I have identification.
They don't even know who the hell I am.
Back to my feet with cuffs on my wrists.
Some discussion with officers,
I still don't believe this.

Cuffs taken off but pain and scars remain.
These officers must be insane.
Now they want to speak with respect,
when a second ago you were trying to break my neck.
No apologies and a quick exit.
I stand there alone and what am I left with?
Scars,
both internal and ex,
and the constant worry of when it will happen next.

FAT BOY!

FAT BOY!

The vilest words ever spewed from the mouth of a now hated villain,
that was once a revered classmate.
FAT BOY!

Disgraced and ashamed,
of being a...
FAT BOY!

Hours standing in the mirror,
hating myself.
FAT BOY!

13 years old taking diet pills
because I hated being a...
FAT BOY!

Rubber suits and steam rooms as a child,
because I despised being a...
FAT BOY!

Wondering if daddy loved me,
because I was too fat to play shortstop!
FAT BOY!

Scared to talk to the girl I loved and who loved me,
because I knew she could not love a...
FAT BOY!

Pain so deep,
it arrests my heart and stifles my ability to reason.
FAT BOY!

continued on next page

continued from preceding page

Seeking solace in my one love,
the food that made me a...
FAT BOY!

A grown man filled with doubt and fear,
not knowing my worth because I was still a...
FAT BOY!

Recognizing that God has love,
for even a...
FAT BOY!

Trying to love my obesity,
finding that to be the dysfunction of a...
FAT BOY!

Health, happy, and fit,
I still think of myself as a...
FAT BOY!

Trying to find the truth,
and constantly fighting the thought that I am a...
FAT BOY!

The Gift and the Curse

If ignorance is bliss,
then I'm in utter despair.
There is such a thing as knowing too much.
There is some beauty in being out of touch.
Is it always a pleasure to be called on in the clutch,
situation?
Frustration,
with my high level of education,
and understanding.
It is a heavy burden to be wise.
Knowledge weighs a lot.
That is why they say, "that's heavy".
It's even heavier when that knowledge is "deep".

It's tedious when it's you they seek,
out,
because something has gone wrong.
When you saw it happening all along,
but they just wouldn't,
or couldn't,
understand.

Now you are called upon to create a new plan,
to manage the detrimental ramifications.
While they are steadily trying your patience,
and there are constantly new faces,
asking the same questions.

"Didn't I just answer that?"
I hate repeating myself.
I repeat,
I hate repeating myself.

continued on next page

continued from preceding page

But it is a necessity,
because I have the knowledge.
And these fools keep testing me,
because my core is peace.
But one question I got for all of ya'll is,
when you gonna open your eyes,
and let the crazy, violent, ineffective, unimpressive, inefficient, nonsense
cease?!

...in due time...

This man I am now,
he troubles me.
But there is a man that I am destined to be,
a man that I will be,
eventually.

...in due time...

I thirst for the future,
but my thirst goes unquenched.
There are trials and tribulations,
in the present tense.

...in due time...

Before I become future perfect,
I must work to remove current imperfections.
Before I am who I will be,
I must BE.

...in due time...

There is so much potential,
so many untold stories.
I yearn to hear the words,
that describe a life that I have lived well.

...in due time...

I ask for patience,
but my patience fails me.
I am bored and frustrated,
with the current challenges that confront me.

...in due time...

continued on next page

continued from preceding page

They are no challenge at all,
I know, that with God's help, all things are possible.
And I long for the day,
when I see myself meet all those possibilities.

...in due time...

He tells me.

Rest

Bury me in sweat pants, house shoes, and cut off sleeves so my tattoo can show.
Inked on chains.
A reminder of bondage,
but now set free.
I am headed home so don't mourn for me.
In fact, I don't need no church walls to contain this party.
I want kegs of beer and half-gallons of Bacardi.
No slow painful songs,
I want guests to hear Ladi-Dadi.
Put the casket out back,
and let's have a cookout.
Let my brother Kendo get on the wheels,
while the Saints pull the book out,
to check for my name.
I want Common and Tupac playin'.
I want an MC to spit a ridiculous verse,
before putting my casket in a Mercedes hearse.
Who would do the eulogy?
Don Magic Juan?
Nah, that ain't me.
Just a moment of silence before they put me in the ground,
let my life speak.
I am now deceased.
So if you got something to say,
speak now or forever hold your peace.

RELATIONSHIPS

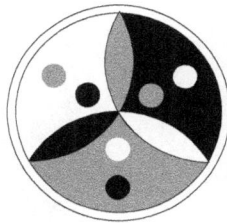

Meet the Parents

Dad was southern born,
in the capital of the Confederacy.
His father was a farmer, contractor, and brick mason,
who placed his sons,
in the fields,
and on the job,
at an early age.
The family valued education,
so as he graduated from high school,
Dad planned his escape to college,
in a quest for knowledge.
More importantly it was a chance to get away,
from the fields and the jobs.
He was driven by fate,
to our nation's capital.
Overwhelmed by the challenge,
and not knowing what came next,
he returned home humble,
seeking another chance.
In Greensboro, North Carolina,
God would place this man.
Seeking education in arts that were industrial,
he found peace in what he knew,
and recognized that he had great skills.
These skills he would harness later,
to become an educator,
and ultimately entrepreneur.
He had a smooth way,
a silver tongue,
and his heart was good,
even if it fell short of pure.

continued on next page

Mom was born in a Grove of Willows,
in the Quaker State.
A northern girl whose skin was light,
caught between two worlds,
Black and White.
Not fully accepted in either,
some of her peers despised her.
Mostly because of their jealousy,
of her brilliance and beauty.
Attempts were made by others to deny her opportunities.
But she had a strong will,
a gift from her mother.
And she was highly motivated,
like her sisters and brothers.
These people,
and a mentor-educator,
would give her the tools to achieve great success later.
Off to college she went,
even if it was only her who believed,
in her success.
As athlete and scholar she did achieve.
And when the opportunity arose,
home she did leave.
In Philadelphia, PA and Camden, NJ,
she taught young minds about grammar and diction,
in English and Spanish she taught poetry and fiction.

continued on next page

continued from preceding page

In the Garden State is where they collided,
the combination of two powerful forces with no direction decided.
They saw in each other their hopes and dreams,
careers, homes, children, and they both chose to believe.
Careers, homes, and two children they did have.
Cleveland, Ohio and New York, they did live.
They settled on Teaneck, New Jersey for the dream house and kids.
Two boys they had,
four years apart.
My brother and I were given,
a very good start.

Sometimes the road turns in a way we can't predict,
Mom never truly knew her level of beauty and brilliance.
Dad never really learned how to share or release control.
And these issues,
when combined with a failure to communicate,
made their marriage turn cold.
By this time I was twelve years old.
And with all the fussing and fighting I was glad to see them separate.
Four years later and having moved to Richmond, VA,
Dad had grown very sick,
and was finally called home.
Mom stayed at home,
In Teaneck, NJ,
In the house where my brother and I were raised.
Today she grows older,
but each day she learns,
of her own beauty and brilliance.
While some harsh memories of her life still remain,
she now grows in God's love,
and allows the Lord to remove her pain.

Big Brother

I was born into this world with a guardian angel.
He came four years before to set the stage for,
the coming of his little brother.
There was no other,
that could have done what he did.
He was chosen by God,
to lead the way.
He was there for me then,
and he's still there to this day.

He's my John the Baptist,
and my King David.
The man in the wilderness who told of the coming,
and the Boy King anointed by God.

A warrior.
An artist.
A leader.
A prophet.
Men don't usually express this type of affection,
but I can't stop it.

He kept me alive,
sheltered me from harm.
Provided me with peace,
in the middle of a storm.

He really raised me,
from a boy to man.
No doubt in my mind,
it was part of God's plan.

continued on next page

continued from preceding page

He was his brother's keeper,
no Cain and Abel.
He paved the way,
so I was able.
To go on in life,
to be the man,
that I am today.
Hope he can understand.

The things I have,
and all that I do.
Are largely because of him,
so they are his too.

Love-Hate Relationship

It is love and hate,
the way we relate.
It was love at first sight.
Love at first bite.
I met you at an early age.
Introduced to your tasteful ways.
Sweet, salty, warm, or cold,
it was you I would hold.
I called on you during my lonely nights.
When others rejected me,
I held you tight.
When it was time to celebrate,
you were the life of the party.
By the time I was ten or twelve you were a part of me.
It was then that I began to feel your heavy burden.
The jokes of my peers,
the pain and the tears.
For years,
we went back and forth.
I would try to set boundaries to limit you,
but then I would want more,
and I would let you through.
The summer of ninety-two,
I unknowingly rejected you,
when I truly felt loved.
In college I left you to spend time with my drinking,
and my buds.
As I got older I tried to balance my time with you,
with frequent trips to health clubs.
But the older I got the more you hurt me.

continued on next page

continued from preceding page

Soon I felt like I was carrying a 100-pound weight,
and I realized that the relationship we had was a mistake.
I asked God to put us both in our proper place.
I know I can't live life without you.
I know if I see you too much you will kill me.
For me,
this is life's greatest challenge,
managing this relationship to stay alive.
It seems like it has always been love and hate,
between food and I.

Portrait

Black man.
Wrinkled face bares the worries of fifty-seven years.
Standing in the doorway of an abandoned building.
Pouring rain.
Leaning with despair.
Wondering about tomorrow.
Praying for something to change.
Brown corduroy sport coat.
Black hooded sweatshirt underneath.
He uses it to keep out the pain,
and keep in the little bit of warmth that his frail, thin frame generates.
Warn jeans.
Old, once white, sneakers.
A thick grey beard holds months of struggle.
Winter's coming.

Do You

You pseudo-neo-soul,
wanna be hip-hop,
tryin' to be hot.
Striving for something you're not.
Your second hand clothes don't give you soul.
Only little holes,
in you attire,
that mirror the holes in your soul.
You can't fill those up by trying to be someone else.
You ain't me, nor are you the Mighty Mos Def.
You the almost always left,
behind,
the cutting edge,
you follow closely.
Trying to guess the new trend.
Never a trend setter.
Your soul remains fettered.
Unable to grow,
'cause all you know,
is what is currently "off the chain".
But you fail to see the stains,
you run from the pain,
and seek out a means other than God,
to maintain.
But that all fails to provide you,
with piece of mind.
The sad part is that you're not blind.
You just live with your two eyes closed.
Your third eye has glaucoma,
from the lack of use,
and emotional abuse.

continued on next page

continued from preceding page

You seek a truce,
with the status-quo.
Never seeking to understand what you don't know.
Each attempt you take towards success,
leaves you out of breath,
and one step closer to death.
Don't let it be in vain.
Don't deny your pain.
Embrace it.
Face it.
Taste it.
Own it.
Enjoy it.
'Cause the pain means you're alive.
Pain means you're in God's eyes.
God just wants acknowledgement.
God just wants recognition.
And a place for him in your vision,
of who you are, were, and plan to be.
And whoever that is,
it is beautiful,
as long as you ain't trying to be me!

Thug Life

This beef is genuine.
You sweet like Genuwine.
This heat is genuine.
Say hello to a friend of mine.

You ain't no Scarface.
You ain't Cubano.
Nor are you really a drug lord.
Let's go mano a mano.

Tired of all slick talk,
fools actin' all breezy.
Tired fools actin' all hard,
when they life is so easy.

They got,
food and shelter,
healthcare and education.
So, why you so mad?
Why you so impatient?

Many have it much worse,
and still stay peaceful.
You will have it much worse,
if you listen to these fools.

Talkin' 'bout they thugged out life.
Why would you wanna be a thug?
You should love your life.
Love your wife.
Love your kids.
Love your friends and fam.
Even love your enemies,
THAT'S what makes you a man.

Confusion

Confusion,
is what you cause.
My mind, my soul,
my spirit, my body.
I don't know how to be.
To act.
So I'm just being myself,
and I see how you react,
and how I vibe with you.
I don't know what to do.
I never felt so comfortable.
So at ease.
Please don't leave.
I know you wouldn't,
but I had to say it.
Sometimes at night,
I have to pray it.
Don't get me wrong,
I'm not trying to play with you.
I'm just doing what I feel.
Trying to find out the real deal.
No one has ever left me like this before.
Quite awestruck, but not feeling abused.
Feeling wonderful,
but ever so confused.
Even Jealousy,
confuses me.
He is my enemy,
but constantly knocks at my door.
I open it and invite him in,
to share my time with him.

continued on next page

continued from preceding page

Not to mention,
Passion,
Fondness,
Spirituality,
and Conflict,
who have been my constant companions since "that day".
Still I live my life.
I do the things that the physical world requires of me,
but there is another side of me.
A side in constant struggle for truth,
for an understanding of "this."
On this side I am not followed and consoled,
by my usual friends of Confidence and Security.
No.
Now Confusion is always near me.
I try to shrug him off,
but just at the moment I loose him,
I hear someone else knocking.
It is Jealousy and Passion and they bring Confusion with them.
But I am going to act as if Confusion isn't here,
and spend time with the others who come to visit.
Those who are positive.
Feel the vibe.
Do what Destiny and Nature require of me,
and in the end Confusion will be nothing more than an idea,
or a distant relative who never calls on me.
I guess I will just be,
and see what becomes of me.

US

How can I profess,
my love for you?
I thought you knew,
that the things I do,
are never meant to hurt you.
Words can never tell you,
how I feel for you;
but here I sit,
using them again.
Hoping you can feel my soul,
when you hear them.
I now plan my life for US.
From now on there is no you or me,
only US.
Like that lighting of the Unity Candle,
I said I did not like.
I now feel,
our special light.
A flame eternal,
in our hearts and souls.
A flame that burns forever,
a story untold.
The words are not working.
I need to touch you.
I need to show you.
I am so glad you love me the same way,
so you can understand.
I told you a while ago I had a plan,
now I see it come to fruition.
You must know,
I'm a man on a mission.
A mission of love,
to create a space for US,
and OURS.

continued on next page

I hope that you can feel my power.
I feel yours.
It is awesome.
Your love astounds me.
And you still my homey.
Baller,
shot caller,
playa-playa,
I can't fade ya.
Your always a part of me.
You've reached the heart of me.
I am nothing without you.
And for this reason,
I will never doubt you.
I burn to hear your voice,
I have no choice.
US has taken control of you and me.
So with my plan I will follow through.
There is still one thing I wish I could do,
and I'll make it plain.
I want to take away your pain.
Please tell me how,
I'll do it now.
Whatever it might be.
'Cause this isn't about you or me.
This is about US.
I promise to trust,
Until,
ashes to ashes,
dust to dust,
we leave this world together,
and enter into heaven,
two souls side by side,
linked eternal,
transcending all boundaries,
even the physical.

continued on next page

I see it in your eyes when I look at you.
Absence makes the heart grow fonder,
but it also plays tricks on the mind.
Please remember that we share one,
heart and mind,
soul also included.
Each 180 degrees,
completing our cipher.
Each speaking a testament,
to the rest of our lives together.
So know how I feel,
even though I can't really express it.
And yes!
Our love will be tested.
But let me know,
what's on your mind,
and in your heart,
and I will compromise.
I'll do whatever need be,
to support,
not me,
not you,
but US.

Healing

So in love.
So deep.
So blind.
Wanting to make another happy.
Wanting to fix her problems.
Wanting not to be alone.
Fearing being alone.
Fearing myself.
Fearing failure.
Fearing the world viewing me as a failure.
Accepting the pain.
Accepting the emotional abuse.
Accepting the idea that I am not worth more.
Accepting that her needs are more important than mine.
Pushing to make it work.
Pushing to help her.
Pushing to stay together when she wants out.
Hating the loneliness.
Hating the pain of separation.
Hating the feeling of failure.
Hating being broken.
Hating the move from a 2,000 square foot house to an 8 by 10 room.
Hating the lack of intimacy.
Hating the lack of affection.
Appreciating the peace of solitude.
Appreciating the calm.
Appreciating the ability to do what I choose.
Appreciating the removal of crisis.
Appreciating the opportunity to live.
Appreciating the opportunity to redefine.
Appreciating the opportunity to better myself.

continued on next page

continued from preceding page

Longing for a new life.
Longing for a new love.
Longing for a new hand or face to touch.
Longing for a new one to hold.
Waiting for a new love.
Waiting for more understanding.
Waiting for the fulfillment each passing day brings.
Waiting for God to reveal his plan to me.
Thanking the Lord for being so good to me.

Circles

Another flow,
still no dough.
My wife's crazy ways got me looking at the front door.
Now I am alone,
and on my own.
The New Testament tells me to go,
and live in peace,
find a place for the drama to cease.
Three months on my own,
nine months on my own.
Me, my couch, and ESPN,
so I'm in the zone.
Trying to build a better me,
'cause only I can do me,
you feel me?
Heal me,
Lord,
from the bitterness and pain.
Guide me,
Lord,
to a place that is sane.
Finally some rest.
Finally some calm.
Finally the remotes in my palm.
Alarm rings.
Time for work.
It's all good though.
You know how that go.
Gotta get that dough.
"Gotta get that paper dog".[5]
Hangin' with women,
but let's be friends.

continued on next page

continued from preceding page

No more sex.
No more craziness.
No more spending just my ins.
This is kinda phat.
just chillin' with female friends.
Not chasin' skirts.
No chance of gettin' hurt.
But here is a new friend.
She seems mad cool.
Yeah I remember her from like 97,
back in school.
Good conversation,
her destination,
to visit her girlfriend,
who lives near my location.
Placing us both in a new context together.
More time together.
Drop her off at the airport,
she catches her flight.
I hop in my ride and head back to my life.
But then it hit me,
my heart no longer so light.
Actually quite heavy.
How could this be?
That I now want to spend time with someone,
other than me.
Am I ready?
I don't remember this feeling.
I am just out of a marriage,
and I've done some good healing.
Something so appealing.
Something so sublime.

continued on next page

continued from preceding page

It's not your booty, it's your beauty.
She's a spiritual dime.
A little confusion.
Lord,
"You got me going in circles, round and round".[6]
But that is how the earth go.
Spinning on axis.
I know you hear me Lord,
so I ask you this,
try to guide me away from what's wrong.
Make me wise.
Help make me strong.
Try to guide me away from what's wrong.
Help me be happy.
Show me my path.
Lord be my guide in whatever I do.
Once again my feelings got me shook.
Lord God,
please see me through.

[5] Carter, Sean. (1998). From the song *Paper Chase*. On the album *Vol. 2: Hard Knock Life*. Roc-a-fella Records.

[6] Peters, Jerry & Poree, Anita. (1969). From the song *Going in Circles*. Originally peformed by The Friends of Distinction.

Beats, Rhymes & Us

We make
beautiful
music
together.
The jazz
and R&B.
The groove
and sway.
I want to put
us
on wax.
To spin
and blend.
A sweet mix
of Donny Hathaway
and Mary J.
A pure expression.
Nothin' fake.
No feeling of hate.
Straight love.
Straight
from God on high.
No drugs needed to fly.
To soar. To pour
out my soul.
Into you.

continued on next page

continued from preceding page

Microphone check 1, 2.
The beat drops.
The bass knocks.
Here comes the hip-hop.
Non-stop
emotion.
Floatin'.
Coastin'.
To keys, strings, and horns.
Word is born.
You got me open.
We make
beautiful
music
together.

My Queen

Stephanie Washington Friend is a Queen because she…

Is divinely appointed by God to do the things she is doing.
Accepts tremendous leadership responsibility.
Works to excel at all she does.
Has a giving heart.
Is a superb diplomat.
Carries herself with grace and dignity.
Always thinks about what is in the best interest of her Kingdom.
Is working to improve herself, her Kingdom, and the people around her.

I love Stephanie Washington Friend because she is a Queen.

FAITH

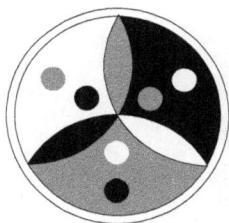

Faith

Now faith is the substance of things hoped for,
the evidence of things not seen.
-- Hebrews 11:1

I walk in darkness,
but I fear no evil.
As I sin,
I recognize that there are unseen consequences to my ungodly ways.
The choice is mine to make.
Will I doubt that God sees my sin?
Would a good father leave his child unpunished for actions they both
    know are wrong?
No.
I believe.
I know.
That the Father cares for me.
He will correct my evil ways.
He will reward my patience.
We will provide my needs.
I walk in darkness.
Even in darkness I move boldly and confidently forward.
He is a light unto my path.
Even in darkness I know that my steps are guided.
Even in darkness I know that I shall not fall.
I am downtrodden.
Beaten.
Exhausted.
Fatigued.

continued on next page

continued from preceding page

At this moment I remain completely dependent on you God.
I acknowledge that there is a plan for me.
Though I may not know it.
It is there.
Thought I may not see it.
It is there.
Though I may not feel it.
It is there.
Though I can not touch it.
It is there.
Though I can not hear it.
It is there.
You are there.
In my weakness, you are made strong.
I know that, despite my weakness, I have strength in You.
I know that I will not be confined by the limits of my knowledge.
I hope for the future.
I know the there are blessings waiting there for me.
I know that You have prepared a place for me.
Although it remains unseen.
I know that it has substance.
Your great works are the only evidence I need.
You are God.
"Goodness in life goes to those who believe.
So I believe." [7]

---

[7] Smith, D. (1999). From the song *Fear Not of Men*. On the album *Black on Both Sides*. Rawkus Records.

Hope

I can't see my future.
I can only see what is right before me.
Like a path into eternity,
lit only by the light of God in my heart.

There is enough light to ensure that I see the footprints on the path.
They are the footprints of Christ.
I hope that if I follow in them,
if I stay on the path of Christ,
I will prosper.

I know there is something,
some place,
some person,
some life,
for me on this path.
But I can only see what is before me.

And so I hope.

For in this hope we were saved. But hope that is seen is no hope at all.
Who hopes for what he already has?
-- Romans 8:24

Love

So many songs about love,
so many psalms about love.
How could I possibly write something strong about love?
But that is one of the beauties of love,
the fact that it appears weak.
Love will inherit the earth,
because love remains meek.
Love covers all,
and rejects not one.
It is the love of a heavenly father,
sacrificing his only begotten son,
for the benefit of the rest of human kind.
Love heals the sick.
Love gives sight to the blind.
Love has nothing to do with candy and flowers.
Love is timeless and could care less about minutes or hours,
day, weeks, months, years, decades.
Love last forever.
Love never fades.
Love never doubts.
Love never fears.
Love continues through pain.
Love continues through tears.
Love will always win,
and love never fails.
Pitted against any other force in the universe,
love always prevails.
Love won't be found in any possession.
Love won't be found in a soul you call your mate.
Love won't be found on any type of date.
Love is not found in a spouse who is true.
Love is not found in your newborn child,
or in anything you do.

continued on next page

continued from preceding page

Faith, hope, and love,
now these three remain.
Love resides above all,
on a spiritual plain.
Love is possessed by the Father,
and to his children freely given.
In spite of any faults you may have, he truly loves you,
But please, now, ask yourself,
"Do I truly love him?"

In Praise of Him

Sittin' in my pew,
prayin' to You.
Lettin' the gospel hit my ear,
makin' me lift my hands in the air.

I'm a quarter century in age now.
You've blessed me to be alive,
and unincarcerated.
It's funny I'm only 24 and I'm broke,
but I feel like I've made it.
It must be stated,
for the record,
that it is You who got me here.
Strengthened my faith,
told me the truth,
and crushed my fear.

The Son of God you are,
or must be to carry me this far.
It seems to me like You have always carried me.
I guess that is what that one set of footprints must be.

You are the perfect example of a man,
it's true.
In every situation,
I try to do what You would do.
Try to be like You.
I know I never will be,
because I was born imperfect,
but Your love has always been perfect.
This life is my job,
and I work it,
for You, My Father.
Why bother with things that pull me away from you?
Whatever You say is next for me, I will do.

continued on next page

continued from preceding page

Still, through these imperfect eyes and tainted soul,
I search for truth.
When I find it I know it's so,
I don't need proof,
or scientific evidence,
when your great love for me is evident.

I will try to be a good reflection of your grace,
for the brief time that I occupy this space.
And after I leave earth,
when I am done,
I hope to serve You Father,
as your son.
For eternity.
For You have served me like no other.

No other has given their life for me.
I don't know why it has taken me so long to see.
I try to make others see it also,
but they are busy worshipping idols.
Enslaved by the weed, ice, cash, and brew,
they are denying themselves a connection with you.

If they would only take the time to understand.
They can do anything,
when they walk within your plan.
Bringing people out of the midst of crack sales, stray bullets, and gun clappin',
I hope they realize that only You could make that happen.

Though I walk through the valley of the shadow of death,
You still provide my needs and give me breath.

I remain on my knees,
to give praise to You.
And for the remainder of my life,
this is what I will continue to do.

The Commandments

God gave us ten rules.
We messed them up so bad that He sent his Son to model the behaviors.
In an effort to make our lives easier,
God's Son narrowed the list of rules to two.
For this, we killed Him.
After all of this,
God continues to love and care for us.

Sin, Repentance & Redemption

A lie or a misunderstanding?
I board a train toward my downtown hotel.
The question dances in my head as the tracks,

"click-clack"

Did I lie?
Yes.

Why did I lie?
I was scared.

But scared of what?

"click-clack"

Scared of someone being mad at me,
scared of loosing something that is a part of me,
scared of someone being right about the way that they see me.

"Next stop, University City-Big Bend. Doors will open to your left."

"click-clack"

But I didn't feel like I was lying until I was challenged on it.
I didn't lie!
Or am I lying now?
Lying to myself.
To protect the original lie.

"click-clack"

continued on next page

continued from preceding page

Repentance.
Lord God!
Jesus!
Please forgive me!
I repent!
Wash me clean!
Make me whole again!
Restore my purity!
Come and abide in me!

"Next stop, 8th and Olive"

I exit to the left,
And re-enter reality.

What have I learned?
I am indeed a sinner.
The devil is a liar!
And he will take advantage of me,
whenever I feel doubt or fear.

I have lost touch with God.
That's when Satan has access,
to use me as his tool.
He did it today and I played the fool.

But I returned to my hotel,
forgiven and redeemed.

And now I pen this lesson,
for others to receive.

Crazy!

In the hustle and bustle I am losing my mind,
seeing the divine and the sublime in a chance to unwind.
My free time is no longer free.
However, while constantly occupied,
I am allowed to be me.
So ultimately,
I am released from the stress and anxiety of the grind,
I am saved from the constant assault on my peace of mind,
generally caused by the hectic pace of a life trying to get it.
I've handed my mind over and now accept it for what is.

"Ha, Ha, Ha…bless your soul.
Do you really think you're in control?
Well I think you're crazy!" [8]

The words gnarl my mind into a place of peace,
I understand my options are to fight or to release.
I should be working on developing a contract,
according to my employer;
but my Lord implores me to follow the will of no one but him.
And as I further submit to his will,
I find that his yoke is easy and his burden is light.
So instead of a constant fight,
I work so that my life brings him delight.
I am loosing my mind;
but that is because it is freely given (along with my body and spirit),
to the one in whom I have complete faith.
I Am.

[8] Burton, Brain; Callaway, Thomas; Reverberi, Gianfranco; Reverberi, Gianpiero. (2006). From the song *Crazy*. On the album *St. Elsewhere*. Originally performed by Gnarls Barkley.

Untitled

Self-hate,
is the debate,
that captures my fate.
Staring in the mirror,
these issues I contemplate.
Stuck inside a life,
I wish I could escape.
It seems that, even in my sleep,
these thoughts tend to penetrate,
my mind state.
Seeking,
equilibrium.
Hoping my peers get the messages,
I'm sendin' em.
Watching more TV and hoping it's,
diversion.
Hoping that the lessons the Lord teaches me,
I'm learnin' em.
Pain roots itself somewhere deep inside me.
Struggling with the thought that once a man could,
buy me.
Try me,
if you don't value what your given.
I won't take a life.
That just ain't how I'm livin'.
Praying to God that there is paradise.
Hoping that to reach it,
I don't have to lose my life.
Self-improvement is what I strive to do.
But I can't quit smoking,
so who I'm tryin' to fool.
Realizing that I am lonely and want someone to love.
But then I'm alone again and all I love is my dub's.

continued on next page

continued from preceding page

Weed sacks and rims,
fly jeans and Timbs,
Stacys and Kims,
Lexus, Jeep, and Benz,
are what I'm found lusting for.
Only without lust,
can I be something more,
or someone even better.
Only with these things gone,
will my soul grow unfettered.
Trying to be like Christ,
but stuck with only being human.
Faced with many sins,
and trying hard to lose em.

What's Good?

What's good son? Is the greeting on the block,
where the crime don't stop,
and the guns go pop.
Every other day another man they slay.
I'm down on my needs and to God I pray.
"I need an escape Lord, I gotta find a way out".
I'm 12 years old and my parents, they just stay out,
on the street,
holdin' heat,
or lookin' for a quick high.
Another day goes by,
I know I'm gonna die,
unless you got my back.
I stay strapped,
with the word,
not the gat.
Haters catch a heart attack.
When we role through, Lord.
Me and you, Lord.
Thought they knew, Lord.

You've been so good to me Lord,
You've been so good to me Lord,
Jesus Christ, he's just nice,
He's what's good!
He's what's good!

Fear Not

Why should I doubt?
Why do I doubt?
Are you not God?
When life gets hard,
I find myself moving towards doubt and fear.
I find my instinct is to resort to tears.
I chase hope away.
I struggle to find a way,
to make it through the day.
What am I afraid of?
Being alone,
being left with no one to protect me.
With no place to go and hide.
With no shelter or fortress to go inside.
I have chosen doubt and fear.
Hope and faith are freely given,
and then I receive instructions from him.
Right there in Isaiah 41:10,
"Fear thou not; for I am with thee: be not dismayed; for I am thy God: I will
strengthen thee; yea, I will help thee; yea, I will uphold thee with the right
hand of my righteousness."
Now I choose faith.
I know I am protected.
I know I am safe.
Fear cannot control me.
I know I have no reason to fear,
for God has told me.

VICTORY!

I now walk with a new sense of peace.
All my doubt and fear, I have released.
I have given it over to Him who died for me.
So that I might have life, and have it more abundantly.

Each morning I wake and give thanks.
For this is the day that He has made.
So I will rejoice and be glad in it.
For the cost of sin has already been paid.

I then submit and ask that I be used to do His will.
As I begin to dress and prepare for my day,
I have no concern about what path to take.
For it is He who will make a way.

As I prepare to break fast,
and give thanks for the food,
I have no concerns about money or need.
For it is not man but Him who provides them to me.

He giveth each day my daily bread.
He forgiveth my trespasses,
as I forgive those who trespass against me.
For He is the Kingdom, and the power, and the glory.

Forever and ever, my life remains in peace.
Despite the heavy traffic I continually seek,
his presence in my morning commute.
For I know He is found by those who seek.

As the challenges of the day begin to press on those around me,
I smile with joy and peace while chaos surrounds me.
No matter what challenge seems to confront me,
the outcome is good, for in Him I have the victory!

Lessons Learned

Dedicated to Sean Christian Cady on December 25, 2008

Patience is a virtue.
Peace is a blessing.
Knowledge is power.
God is good,
all the time.
The world is not of God.
We are in the world.
We can choose to be of the world or not.
Having worldly things does not make you a sinner.
Loving worldly things makes you a sinner.
Faith, hope and love always remain.
Above all of these is love.
Fear not, for God is with you.
Fear is directly opposed to faith.
If you choose faith, you will always find joy.
Faith always defeats fear.
Hope always defeats doubt.
Love conquers all.
If you live your life the way God desires, you will prosper,
and you will always find joy.
If you live your life the way you desire, you will struggle to find joy.
Be thankful for what you **have**.
Ask God to supply what you **need**.
Don't **want** anything.
You are a child of God.
You are more valuable than any material thing.
You are as valuable as any other human being.
You are loved.
You have the greatness of God inside of you.
If you surrender to God it will come out.
Walk in it!